Songs from the Black Hole

poems by

Loretta Oleck

Finishing Line Press
Georgetown, Kentucky

Songs from the Black Hole

*For my father,
Theodore Sargent Oleck
a mischievous spirit, somewhere out there,
in the great unknown*

Copyright © 2016 by Loretta Oleck
ISBN 978-1-63534-088-4 First Edition
All rights reserved under International and Pan-American Copyright Conventions.
No part of this book may be reproduced in any manner whatsoever without written permission from the publisher, except in the case of brief quotations embodied in critical articles and reviews.

ACKNOWLEDGMENTS

*Comets: originally published in *Marco Polo Arts Magazine* in 2012 titled "comets" has been revised for this publication.
*Bones & Stars: originally published in *Gilded Frame: Kind of a Hurricane Press* titled "bones and stars" has been revised for this publication. It was inspired by Francisco Goya's *The Half-Submerged Dog*.
*Orchid Baby: originally published in Mas Tequila Review titled "orchid baby" has been revised for this publication.
*The Synaesthete: originally published in *In Gilded Frame: Kind of a Hurricane Press* titled "the synaestheste" has been revised for this publication.
*Refraction: makes reference to *The Diamond Lens*, a short story written by Fitz James O'Brien.
*The Man in the Moon: Carl Sagan quote from the *Demon-Haunted World*.

Thank you to the talented poets who helped to make this book a reality: the prolific Alexis Rhone Fancher and Matt Bialer who are both daily creative inspirations. Thank you to Robert Kelly who thrilled me with his wise feedback and poetic review, and Barbara Fischer for her beautifully focused comments. I also thank my family and friends: Olivia and Noah Berger, Adrienne Oleck, and Sandra Oleck. Thank you to my creative and eclectic father, Theodore Oleck, to whom this collection is dedicated, for inspiring me to be curious about the cosmos. Thank you to Linton Suttner for supplying the author photos, as well as consistently celebrating all of my creative endeavors.

Publisher: Leah Maines
Editor: Christen Kincaid
Cover Art: Loretta Oleck
Author Photo: Linton Suttner
Cover Design: Elizabeth Maines

Printed in the USA on acid-free paper.
Order online: www.finishinglinepress.com
also available on amazon.com

Author inquiries and mail orders:
Finishing Line Press
P. O. Box 1626
Georgetown, Kentucky 40324
U. S. A.

Table of Contents

Quarks & Leptons 1
Golden Ratio 2
Frida Kahlo, Georgia O'Keefe, Crazy Horse, & All
    the Others 3
The Optimistic Eternalist 5
Raspberries & Rum 6
Comets 7
Orchid Baby 9
Quantum Entanglements 10
The Fermi Paradox 11
Bones & Stars 12
String Theory 13
Star Man 15
Philae & 67P 16
The Firebird 18
Lights 20
Gravedigger 21
Mare Ignotum *(Sea of Mystery)* 22
Under the Midnight Sky 23
Songs from the Black Hole 24
Refraction 25
The Synaesthete 26
The Pawpaw Tree 28
Spirit 29
DNA 31
The Man in the Moon 32
Bridge 33
Blind Men 34

"We are a way for the universe to know itself. Some part of our being knows this is where we came from. We long to return. And we can, because the cosmos is also within us. We're made of star stuff…"

—Carl Sagan

Quarks & Leptons

Particles float like ghost birds in flight
or ribbons of light.

You stroke my belly, thighs, ass—

an invisible field of energy
imbuing particles with mass.

I feel it—

our own private cosmos
existing before your caress
and long afterwards too.

That slow rake of your nails
that turns complacency into shivers
along the ladder of my spine.

You say *quarks* and *leptons* are not sexy words
but there's a sexiness in that they mate for life.
Indivisible.

I fear we are breaking into less
than what we have been. Surely,
this weight is elusive enough
to avoid detection.

I remind myself—
we are always more than our mass.

Golden Ratio

Climbing the spiral staircase, I travel through a helix,
through hidden strands of DNA, along the revolving ridges
of a nautilus, reaching a checkerboard room of floor to ceiling
stained glass windows changing hues with each season.

There you are, with abacus beads of sweat dripping
down your back, measuring two equal panes of glass,
dividing one in half, swinging a compass downwards,
then tapping the intersection of diagonal and base.

This is where your bed stands draped in a sunflower quilt.

This is where we fold together—origami bodies among petals
and strings of pearls, lit only by the glow of a blood moon
winking through sky-lights.

And when it rains we sleep curled inside the open mouth
of a drum or between the puckered lips of a heart.

I place my ear to your wrist listening to the ocean's hum:
stars above earth below stars above earth below,

trying to decipher an arithmetical solution
to freeze frame this very moment.

But time is a magician playing with perception,
using sleight of hand to command the universe
to expand faster than the speed of light.

One moment, we fiercely tumble in your bed.
The next moment, we vanish.

My bones ache with this coming together and pulling apart—

a sequence and a motion found even in the tiniest seeds
spiraling round the brightest head of a sunflower.

Frida Kahlo, Georgia O'Keefe, Crazy Horse & all the others

My clock wears a cherry red shawl,
the one I knit on our first summer at the Cape.

The one that draped over the naked breasts
of another woman young enough to be our daughter—

the two of you behind a lolling dune with bodies
braided and elongated like tousled seaweed.

My clock became an inconsolable Frida Kahlo
whose broken bones moaned under plaster,
before time stood still and peeling paint revealed
the underbelly of a most unexpected universe.

You said—
She meant nothing. The past no longer exists.
Choose to live in the 'now.'

I tried choosing the *now*—
living in between what was and what would be,

tightening my grasp on your hands that had long ago
swung a lasso capturing the wildest of our days
and taming them into submission. Hands that gripped
the reins of a Pinto and galloped through the lushness
of my hidden tangled forest.

Hands that would shockingly betray.

But my clock was ticking with potential—
an unrestrained Georgia O'Keefe posing nude for your clock
named Stieglitz, Diego Rivera, or John Wayne.

Didn't matter which, just so long as our tick tock
matched up in synchronized beats:

one second per one second per one second.

Just so long as we didn't turn our cheeks
from Frida Kahlo, Georgia O'Keefe, Crazy Horse,
and all the others.

But I don't forgive you. I could never forgive you.

So our days have turned to years and we have become
what we promised we would never be.
Or what we always were. What we are today.

Our clocks have grown up and grown wings
with a span as infinite as our history. Feathers as bright
as the lipstick smeared across your cheek.
Red as my knitted shawl.

Our wings wildly flap, splattering paint
and raining down tears as they fly.

Mine—heading South.
Yours—due North.

The Optimistic Eternalist

When was our first moment—the one we defined as our beginning?
Was it when you found me asleep on a bed of muted sea-glass?
When you were Jack climbing the beanstalk to retrieve our golden egg?
The day the universe was created?

What happened before the Big Bang?

I stand naked flipping a runny omelet. The yolk—a sun
concealed inside the secret world of a newly laid egg,
plucked from under the belly of a free-range chicken,
who got it on with a cocky rooster. On a farm. In a biosphere.

Infinite hands of time meet right here—
our past beginning before we met.
Happening now. Lasting forever.

You are upstairs thinking of ways to break up with me,
as if you have the power to create an end, shooting out
bullet points of my faults then weighing their mass.

But I will not disappear.

I am an *eternalist* who can simultaneously crack an egg shell,
flip an omelet, make love in the garden of Eden, lie on my deathbed
(a mattress stuffed with the downy fullness of my mistakes)—
all of that, while being birthed with wide-eyed optimism,
13 billion years from now.

Raspberries & Rum

In dark pockets of the universe linger scents
of jasmine tea, gunpowder, seared steak—

your hair smells like rum and we sit too close
for comfort.

You are my ex-husband's wife—
all 37 trillion cells of you have stepped
into my boots, tasted my food, slept
under my quilt.

I see myself reflected in your eyes,
the me I was twenty years ago,
before my journey to Sagittarius B2—
the giant dust cloud in the heart of the Milky Way
where *ethyl formate* spreads across my tongue,
tasting like raspberries, smelling like rum—

the fragrance of your hair.

You pull up a chair but I have no time
for idle chit-chat. I am filled with the hubris
of a hunter hunting down the building blocks of life—

my life/your life/all of our lives/overlapping,

amino acids, molecules, chemicals—
fingerprints braided together making it near impossible
to disentangle one from the other.

You are me when I was younger, and I am your future—
one you could never imagine possible
from 27 thousand light years away.

It comes down to rum and raspberries
closing the gestalt of our lives.

It is only now, being older, that I understand
a shooting star is birthed inside a dust cloud.

Comets

Even in the light of a solstice moon
you didn't see the ruins strewn
inside my shaky mind—
a hidden mine field behind my mask
of feeling fine.

Just fine.

You didn't find the sleeping wolf,
the weeping self, the skipping heart.

How could you know?

Your touch was a rush. Your lush whisper—
a marked trail leading me away from the cold,
the fear, the numb, scared tears, from the me
covered up in Jungian myth, and shit.

I saw a shooting comet last night
above your hammock in your personal patch
of dusky night sky, and I could've cried
when it disappeared because we *always* disappear—
into ourselves, into the earth, into our fears,
into our self-proclaimed worth.

We are two quiet comets tumbling
towards each other in space, not uttering
a word of what we don't want to face.

*A gospel kind of love making,
an earth shaking, be kind to yourself,
be kind to me awakening.*

*But the closer we come,
the warmer we feel,
and the warmer a comet,
the more it melts
into nothing.*

Orchid Baby

She said—
My internal eco-system is fragile.
I'm an orchid baby. Handle me with care.

She's a single Vanda orchid propped and pinned
at all the points where her spine like a stem
might snap or curve into weakness.

Oh yeah, she's an orchid baby, alright,
with milky thighs and petal eyes.

Her eco-system balances on a tightrope
between a spinning earth and stunning stars,
shooting up the echo of ego into open veins.

With one hand, she raises a shield to keep me out
while she wields a spear with the other
in an attempt to make her terror disappear.

Raising orchids is an art, and I'm no artist, baby.
I can't pitch a stake to hold you up or water you
with chips of ice.

You're too preoccupied with how to stay alive
to notice that I am gone.

Quantum Entanglement

We hold on, for dear life, to the *Higgs boson* particle
hurling through forces carrying atoms, creating mass,
bouncing between time and space like a tossed ball
in a child's game of jacks.

Our resistance and insistence accelerate
by the strength of our attraction.

Our passion is a stone skipping along the surface of a pond—
revealing the outermost edge of your sighs racing towards
the innermost parting of thighs.

When you pull out, and away, you say—
Relax, baby, we will always be one.
What happens to you, happens to me.

But because the skin of the stone clings to my bone,
unashamed and untamed, impenetrable and unrestrained,
I am certain we are not one. We are not protons hurling
through space.

We come together, venture out solo, then return once again,
to our marshy unmade bed where we have spent light years
waiting for the ball to bounce, the jacks to tumble,
the greedy sweep of hands to fumble.

We come face to face with random symbols—
nimble stones dropping from *God particle's* palm—
shiny metal jacks strewn across galaxies.

If you are right, and we are *one*, then our veins are worm-holes,
and I taste your blood while licking my wounds.

The Fermi Paradox

Shirtless, he shows me the scratches,
the powdery patches, the burns, the light glowing
from tight wires inserted and bound under his skin.

He digs a paper clip in between two toes.
Don't you see? Rows of cable wedged deep inside?

On the table, he fans out photos of Tibetan beads,
Hubble images, the crack of his ass, moldy flesh.

I scrubbed the mold off with bleach, he says.
See the carpet—those black threads were never there before.

You know, he says, *when Enrico Fermi gazed at the night sky
and asked, Where is everybody? I could've told him
there's no paradox in proof—*

*extra-terrestrials are self-reproducing like bacteria
sending signals through worm holes, playing Russian
roulette with my mind.*

I bend down stroking the carpet threads
that he insists were never there before today,
and my body suddenly quivers with the charge
of an electric shock.

We believe what we want to believe.

Bones & Stars

Buried dog, half-drowned dog, hidden
between the parched lips of sky and shore,
forever a pale shadow on decaying walls.

The truth is that we are all lost dogs
sniffing for bones and stars, expecting marrow
and fire to be our guides,

*as if without these steering symbols
our lives would be a ride with no purpose.*

It is the truth—or at least a half-baked truth
that Goya was a deaf man who bought
a crumbling villa from another deaf man,
never intending to reveal his silenced pup
painted and stuck on the bare walls of what he called
the *Villa of the Deaf Man*.

A hieroglyphic symbol of the fact that we don't listen—
never hearing the creaking sounds of our aging bones
or the resounding tones of living in the fullness
of each breath.

We exist because an omniscient painter flicked his wrist
splattering colored oil off his brush in a twist and a froth,
birthing us into a single sea tangle, too terrified to dive
through rising waves, too set in our ways to ever be saved.

What we don't understand we reject, becoming as meaningless
as doodad dogs splayed between sky and shore, defeated
by limitations and flaws, with no intention to freely roam,
lost in the futile search for stars and bones.

String Theory

She lives alone hammering spoons
while her mutts bark and bang their heads
sensing thunder rumbling from too far away
for the human ear to hear.

Her husband left and she never saw it coming—
the lightening bolt streaking across the sky,
splitting the old willow and singeing a fringe of leaves,
shattering her window and branding an epitaph
upon her forehead.

She's covered all her mirrors so not to see
the reflection of the wound of words bequeathing her
patron saint of her own universe, where she reconfigures
rusty spoons into chimes, connecting them with fishing wire
to old teapots, sifters, mixers, and keys.

Some have open strings with two end points
like marriage and divorce—two spoons that came together
but never touched, then slipped and landed with a thud.

Some have closed strings forming a loop
where there is no beginning and no end—
holding her creations secure enough to last
through many seasons and storms.

She spends her nights with her ear pressed to the pane,
listening to the chimes vibrate from bowed branches
and metal hooks under eaves,

*remembering Pythagoras's theory—
basic intervals of music are re-created
in the motions of the planets,
giving form and order to everything
in the universe.*

Her dogs wildly bark but it is impossible
to hear what they hear—
the harmonics of tinkling silver, the clunk of metal,
the music of planetary motion, and lightning bolts
that strike when least expected.

Star Man

He says—

*Our bodies are made of dead stars and comets.
I commune with trees. I speak to animals.
I cure disease. We constantly regenerate.*

Joni Mitchell was right—we are stardust.

We are stardust.

He points to a constellation of liver spots
speckled over his arms—

They are sun spots.

He points to my crotch—

*I call that the Nebula—
the place where stars are born.*

He says—

*I want to lick them up and spit them out.
I want to Big Bang you under the Milky Way.*

It will make me feel like God.

Philae & 67P

She is a little probe named Philae—
a descending blue moon etching a path
in the cosmos.

She confides that her wish is to be the constellation
of a grizzly tattooed on my thigh because my skin
is safer than the sky.

At times, she imagines she is a white rabbit
because a rabbit's foot brings luck.

But don't you dare use mine, she says,
to dangle your keys.

She is a tease, unbuttoning her blouse.

She says, *You better make sure my battery never dies.*

Everything lies silent now with only one hour of sunlight
in this ice mountain comet's 12 hour day.

She thinks, *I don't want to stay in this place
that has remained unchanged since the formation
of planets 4.6 billion years ago.*

Everything feels big to her. Big like a big deal with big ideas
weighing her down, and a soft heart palpitating within a galaxy
of rattling bones.

She knows she is being left alone with no more energy
to move forward. But she is a scrappy one—
a tabby with a limp mouse swinging from her mouth.

Neither fueled by hunger nor curiosity
but by time and luminosity.

If her choice is death or hibernation, she will choose
the latter—hunkering down, for as long as it takes,
the only possible means for survival.

Firebird

Past

No one ever asked me anything so I never learned to speak.
I needed to be taught, but no one thought to teach.

I couldn't pull the alarm as it was too far out of reach,
so I was consumed inside an invisible blaze—
an unobserved, exploding Super Nova.

Firefighters never doused the flames. There was no witness.
I made no sound.

Present

Now, I am a fire-bird flying off cliffs. A crimson streak of a bird
with a beak painted blue. A red hot-shot flame of a bird
illuminating the night sky. A constellation.

But my wail is the wail of dark matter drowned out
by the buzz of questions—
Am I alive? Dead? Simultaneously, alive and dead?

It's the observing that creates the outcome.
But who's checking?

No one knows if I am a firebird soaring in space,
or if I am Schrodinger's cat, locked in a steel box,
waiting for the hammer to fall.

Future

The identity of the observer will matter.

If you are my lover, I will offer you a magic feather to light up the dark.
If you are a firefighter, you will have arrived too late.
If you are my voice, then you will have finally found me, and I will use you to question why I was left, all these years, alone, in a box.

I will use you to scream.

Lights

Two light specks spotted on the dwarf planet Ceres—
between Jupiter and Mars, 266 million miles from earth.

One dares to be luminous—a sheet of shiny mica.
The other—dim with muted flares.

I follow the Dawn Spacecraft searching for explanations
while imbuing these two lights with human qualities.

I know them as well as I know the two of us—

I'm the one having a hard time shining in the shadow
of your bedazzling good looks, quick wit, and glorious shimmy
of wide hips in front of the telescope lens, blocking my view,
ravaging my wonder with your fleeting moods spread underfoot.

You are a sheet of thin ice throwing off my balance.
I have fallen so many times that walking has become
no longer natural.

Scientists are puzzled as to the nature of this duo—
inventing theories that are just theories and will remain so
until there are more theories and more complex images
with sharper resolution.

For now, I linger background becoming faint and indistinct—
the only form of protection from your probing eye and sharp tongue.

You are not your appearance—
neither highly reflective rock nor salt from hidden saline seas.
You are myth, vivid fiction, sensational, and false.

Although your bright lights boldly seduce, they are nothing
more than the banal symptoms of a dying star.

Grave-digger

I shuck pistachios and feed them to you, one by one,
so that you can rest under bowed branches of pear blossoms,
and heal your stinging palms, caked in earth, calloused
from daily digging—

ax to edge, loosening topsoil, boot heel to steel,
spade peeling star moss, hacking through tangled roots,
chucking stones into a waiting wheelbarrow.

The deeper you burrow the more facts you mine—

NASA is just two weeks away from a close up look
of the dwarf planet Pluto.
Tonight there will be a leap second where time stands still
and a minute will become 61 seconds.

You reveal stories of stars and time, and revel in the secrets
of those you have buried—

this one was a drifter whose heart gave out,
that one was a painter who hung himself,
a three year old who drowned,
a teacher—a pastor—a mother of six.

I don't want to hear about what looms above
or whom rests below.

I'd rather shuck pistachios and feed them to you, one by one,
as you bury your fingers in a mix of soft pear blossom petals
and coarse shells that changed color, then split open,
as the fruit became ripe.

Mare Ignotum *(Sea of Mystery)*

While deep in sleep
you shift to your left side
(that side that arches and aches
when you strain), tightening
your arm over my waist.

I know that quiet gasp means
you have just set sail.

I
lie
still
awake.

Your arm drape loosens
as you drift farther out to sea—
away from me,
away from language,
away from illusory time.

Whispered words—

sleep well,
g'night,
love you,

lose all meaning as you passage past
that point where there is nothing
left to share,

plummeting over-board
with a sloshing heart composed
of 73% water, disappearing,
over and again, behind closed lids.

The sound of your breath quickens,
traveling faster through water
than through air.

Night after night, I become a buoy,
holding us steady, so we don't drown.

Under the Midnight Sky

Knee pressed hard against rock, edging the flapping fire.
One rubber soled boot melting from heat, the other one
shoved aside in dusty snow. One goose bumped bare leg
buckled over your melon belly, under a swarm of stars—
Great Bear, Big Dipper, Polaris.

Ladybugs flashing in firelight.

Cold earth backing you up, breaking the ice—

damp between night sky and legs.

We were nothing special—a middle-aged couple
with fan-tailed, web-winged eyes, flying through time.

Time—nothing more than the study of change.

Ethereal skin becoming creased and weathered,
glowing tough in the heat. Comet tails tapering off
in the hum of empty space.

Next to the fire, under the stars, you played my body
the same way you played harmonica, blowing and sucking,
flicking tongue licking the smallest holes, the lowest notes,
with the space between tongue and skin swelling
and contracting—

star patterns puffing up, then petering out—
a stretching rubber-band losing elasticity.

Songs from the Black Hole

250 million light years from earth
lives a lone black hole in the center
of the Perseus galaxy—

the whirring heart of the universe,
purring in B flat—
57 octaves below middle C,
singing the same song for 2.5 billion years.

Does sound exist if we don't hear it?

Does love exist if we don't feel it?

Forlorn black holes croon to infinite space,
and to lonesome people, more people than there are stars,
wondering if anyone knows they are alive—

solo divas creating elusive beauty among the cosmos,

I   am   here
 we   are   here

Even with our eyes closed we believe the universe
is filled with echoes of the big bang's tone and harmonics,

the hiss and drone of *M87*—
a galaxy sheltering one of the largest black holes.

Even the sun has been chanting for billions of years.

The existence of song or love is not dependent
upon what we witness.

The hum of heaven is as momentous
as the B sharp buzz of a lone bee
resting on a rose.

Refraction

You are a salesman selling lenses
to researchers hunched over microscopes
viewing translucent zebra fish in Petri dishes,

to astronomers hauling the expanding universe
into a tighter frame, a lighter image,

to those constructing the Giant Magellan telescope
in order to discover exo-planets—others worlds
orbiting single stars.

You tell me a story—*The Diamond Lens:*

*See now, there's this scientist who peers through a microscope.
Lo and behold, he falls in love with the most beautiful woman
living in a secret world inside a single drop of water.*

This story makes me like you.

While you kiss me under the bright street lamp,
your bloodshot eyes are Jupiter-ringed with dark circles,
as if you'd been pressing a viewfinder hard against them
to magnify my pores, my flaws, my pleasure, my pain.

It starts to rain—a single drizzle dripping down my glasses,
bending the light so you appear to be a weeping alien.

What worlds reside within your tears?

If I kiss you longer, harder, looser, would I become
a woman trapped within a single drop of rain?

The Synaesthete

A Kandinskian braille of bump-along trails and willy-nilly symbols
pockmarked with squiggles scrape me inside out.

Your paintbrush tip smudges grey grout inside the creases of my brow,
reality mixes with fairy tale—
a magician with slight of hand caring less about the reason or the subject
and more about the treason or the trick.

Waving your wand makes me disappear. I want you and I don't,
because you've made me into what you think I am.

Cold.

Not crack-the-musical-whip kind of cold,
but more of a cowardly egg yolk, yellow cold—
losing my centered sense of self.

I've learned this from you, and for that, I ask you to beg
for my forgiveness.

You say—
I can't be sorry for what I paint when the color of butter
sounds like middle C on a brassy trumpet, and bare boned
black-black-black taps out our end.

Your painting was once propped on its side before it had fully dried.
You fell to your knees deeply weeping, touched by newly colored signs
and musical lines you had never intended.

The best rises from what we never intended—
revelations tangled in sensations of color.

You
were
released.

Kandinsky—
turn me on. Turn me round on my side. Plunge your hands
and your plans into a pigment that you never intended to drip—
a purple dribble in b major between the ladder of my ribs.

Kandinsky, find something in me you've never found before.

The Pawpaw Tree

I stand tall like a carved arrow aiming for heaven.
My tongue is a heart-shaped leaf settling in my mouth.
It is predestined for me to guzzle up sunlight
and grow taller than the birch and the oak.

Everything is encoded in our core.

It takes 8.3 minutes for the sun's glow to reach and warm my skin,
yet you sat beside me for a full twenty years (over 10 million minutes),
and never plucked a single blade of grass from my graying hair.

You must be dusk itself.
You must be the darkest part of twilight.
You must be the hidden pit inside a blackened plum.

Everything is encoded in our core.

I call you Pawpaw because you are shade tolerant,
able to thrive under a canopy of dimness, roots coiling down
into the acidic soil. You are an understory tree and I loom heavy
over your fruit.

We've missed each other's finer moments—
when you plucked a strawberry moon from the sky,
and flipped it in your mouth like a gumball,
when I sipped black lemon tea under a Shah Toot tree,
when you played Vivaldi's fifth on your violin, and the musical notes
turned to petals blowing like confetti in the breeze.

We, too easily, let each other slip away—

I became an arrow soaring swiftly into the bull's eye of a black hole.
You became the Pawpaw, short under the shadow of taller trees,
deepening your roots underground, with blind worms and chilled
earth surrounding you.

Leaving those we love is part of everything.
And everything is encoded in our core.

Spirit

My home that used to be our home
has just enough permeability
for your spirit to enter and exit
when I'm not looking,

floating from room to room,
around piles of stacked paperbacks
like stone cairns memorializing what once was,

revealing yourself through a breeze
in the otherwise stagnant air.

You smoke when I'm not there.
You smoke often and cry seldom
convinced you are now too good for crying—
being of the spirit world.

You scramble my words into gibberish
when I talk topics you don't appreciate,
molding my tongue as if pushing your thumb
into soft wax, plying my words into something
other than what they are.

I loved you till you began to float instead of walk
with feet no longer tethered to weathered earth—
you rose not as a prophet but more as a cloud
of tiny particles,

not as a power but more as a smokescreen
hiding who you were when you were.

On any given day at any given hour,
your smoke lingers on my clothes,
drips down my hair.

Your moods depend upon your moods,
and my moods depend upon your moods.

I know I have stepped into that place
where living solitary has grown too natural—
I already cannot remember the feel of lips
grazing the contours of my neck.

I no longer regulate my heartbeat or blood-flow
to yours or anyone else's.

You left me alone like a chip of stone
wedged between the teeth of this home—
lonely rooms chomping at the bit,
hungry for the food we used to share.

You and this old house are in cahoots—
cannibals, devouring me, limb by limb.

DNA

You are healed, said the witch doctor
after chanting voodoo over my bowed head,
and rubbing my back in reassuring circles,
repeating *tshay—tshay*.

Was it the surgeon or the voodoo that saved my life,
the candle lit in St. Peter's church,
my whispering prayer to the cosmos,
the born-again who said Jesus knows,
or the swami mantra I hummed in a haze?

Was it the red beaded strands of evil eyes
strung around my wrist and hips,
or plain old luck that did the trick?

Or was it love?

Fear is the opposite of love.
Love is the opposite of fear.

Was it written in the stars—*today's not my day to die?*
Is there a grand scheme of punishment and redemption
when braided together create a cord of illusion called life?

Life, as a pair of molecules bound together like marriage,
a double-helix, a twisted ladder of straining fingers
clutching shared ancestral stories.

Science is imperfect, but DNA doesn't lie.
I will be known and remembered
from just a drop of blood.

The Man in the Moon

> "The Man in the Moon is in fact a record of ancient catastrophes—most of which took place before humans, before mammals, before vertebrates, before multi-celled organisms, and probably even before life arose on Earth. It is a characteristic conceit of our species to put a human face on random cosmic violence."
> —Carl Sagan

My son plays electric guitar with a hard-ass bass beat smacking the spine of the house. My daughter squints through the backyard telescope trying to spot Jupiter—a round circle with 4 fuzzy Galilean moons. Her gaze, instead, settling on the Man in the Moon.

The familiar loses the mask of mundane when something happens- a diagnosis, let's say. Cutting through the hum of home. Filleting flesh. Bending bone.

I listen to old jazz records to still my mind, focusing on words to songs like Mona Lisa by Nat King Cole and Fever by Peggy Lee.

Right before he died, my father said he'd protect me. Forever. He lied. Or didn't want me to know there's nothing but space junk on the other side. No spirits lurking, no angels tweaking harp strings. Nada. Zippo. Zilch.

He's never coming back.

I listen to the scratch of my daughter's pencil sketching images of Super Novas and Great Voids, and the scrape of my son's disposable razor grazing across the peach fuzz sprouting on his adolescent chin.

I hum along with the same tunes, over and again, fixing my eyes on the benevolent face with an open mouthed grin, like a father, my father, pretending to know how to protect his kin.

Bridge

> "God does not play dice with the universe."
> —Albert Einstein

My knees feel weak as I drive over the bridge—
a looming arc waiting at the other end
against the sheerest sheet of stark sky,
with the flutter of pigeon wings beating in my chest.

Up ahead cars speed through the steel bow
then drop out of sight.

My uncle eats anchovies and avocado at the diner,
after his wife's unveiling where a crop of tombstones
moaned and whined side by side for miles.

My uncle says—
*The dead are ships tumbling over the horizon,
no longer visible, yet continuing to exist.*

My uncle has a shock of white hair, Italian leather shoes,
and a pink diamond glittering on his pinky.

At the graveside the rabbi waved his hands
and lifted his voice like a croupier shouting—

*Life is a game—play it!
Life is luck—make it!
Life is an adventure—take it!*

Stumbling forward with wet cheeks and sunken shoulders
my uncle cried out, *Esther!*

The rabbi raised the cheesecloth that covered the stone,
and instead of saying, *Amen*, after Kaddish,
I'm sure I heard, *Ta-dah!*

We each took our turn balancing pebbles on the stone's rim.

Then driving back the same way I came,
I white knuckle the steering wheel as I approach the arc
leading to that place that surely exists, even if impossible to see.

Blind Men

Their fingers flutter across pillars of ivory,
exploring the leathery skin of an elephant
whose spongy feet hold up the great weight
of the universe.

Broken lives tiptoe inside the unbroken.
Nothing whole is whole.

Does an elephant's tongue feel like silk or mortar?
Do blind men make love blindly?

Moths to beams, sleepers to dreams, bishops to knights,
explorers traversing the night. If blind men are wise men,
they will follow the fragrance of the North Star.

Blood smells tart and tastes bitter. Might the death
of planets, stars, earth, also carry tastes and scents?

Pressing lifelines together, they lead each other away
from this great mammal that will surely be extinct
within fifty years time.

Narcissus fell deeply in love with what wasn't there
before tumbling into mourning and despair,

while these blind men rise from mud
above perception, sensation, opinion—
levitating like winged lotuses above oblivion.

The elephant flings hard his trunk, cracking earth,
digging his own grave, where murky rain water
puddles then drains.

What you cannot see does not exist.

Nothing lasts forever.

www.ingramcontent.com/pod-product-compliance
Lightning Source LLC
LaVergne TN
LVHW050045090426
835510LV00043B/3210